Tamaren

David Elkins

Published by The Sole Proprietorship of David Wayne Elkins

Jacksonville, Oregon

2023

1

ISBN-13: 979-8-9897298-8-3

Library of Congress Control Number: 2023916479

Cover design by: David Elkins

Printed in the United States of America

Publisher: The Sole Proprietorship of David Wayne Elkins

Publication Date: August 29, 2023

Place of Publication: Jacksonville, Oregon

Books by the Author

Marakin

Denewen

Nuna Anodm

Table of Contents

Introduction

In Chapter 1 and Chapter 2 social interaction is examined in pertaining to shape and mechanics. In social interaction people gather and form group shapes, carry out mechanical motions, and operate functions.

There is a group of people that form four shapes. They start by forming a circle, then a three-sided structure, a perpendicular corner of two lines, and then a line of people. There are four shapes formed in sequence.

Another group forms a line that diverges into two lines with a passage between that people can traverse. The shapes are the lines and the mechanical motions are the divergence of the lines.

A third group operates a function. Each person in the group utters a sound when a neighbor within 5 feet utters a sound. The sound can propagate in radial, linear, and spiral shapes.

The wielding and exchanging of objects in groups is another area for interaction. Balls, bars, rectangular plates, and other objects may be utilized in group arrangements. The objects can be held or be embedded in the environment to interact with.

A group of people hold rods and objects that are triangular, square, pentagonal, and hexagonal. A person is at each of the tips of the objects. People can hold one of the tips, transit to another tip on the object, or transit to another object if there is an open position. The objects are wielded by the group in different configurations.

In Chapter 3 audio and video devises in the landscape are described. Chapter 4 - Chapter 6 explores the senses, sense organs, navigation, and course charting in the environment. The five senses and other senses may be assisted with apparatus, body wear, and clothing accessories.

An accessory to wear that is an auditory and visual device might be a 3 x 3 array of speakers with an electromagnetic wave detector that emits a sound whenever electromagnetic waves of a frequency range are detected at an intensity in the cell of the array.

Sense can be explored with tools. Ten substances to smell are put on a strip in sequence to move under the nose from left to right. The strip is a tool to describe scents over time.

Chapter 7 goes into locomotion, interaction, and biometrics. Locomotion and mechanics are utilized to move in the environment and operate objects. A man keeps his palms 1 - 2 feet distance a part over a period of 1 hour. For the second hour he keeps his palms 2 - 2.5 feet distance apart. The behavior of distance ranges for palms is mechanics in interaction.

Chapter 8 is on language and computers. The presentation of descriptions of places and events can be conveyed with language. A matrix of numbers, an array of Alphabet letters, and linear sequences of words are descriptions of what may be places, events, processes, and configurations.

To describe an event the description might be linear, two-dimensional, three-dimensional, or more than three-dimensional. The manner of language might be communicated with sound and visual components. Sensory conveyance can occur with many kinds of qualia.

Communication can occur via heat. Thirty heaters are put in a row that can be set to one hundred different temperatures. Each temperature is assigned a language symbol. A person presses their finger on the row of heaters to read the sequence of symbols.

In Chapter 9 clothing and clothing accessories are presented. Physical and mechanical clothing features are diverse. A shirt with a layer of gallium liquid would distributes weight differently than a shirt with a layer of H_2O.

Chapter 10 is on systems of physical, chemical, and geological structures. Such structures might be water gates on a canal, filling of land in water with dikes, water sanitation plants, and reef structures for corals to grow on.

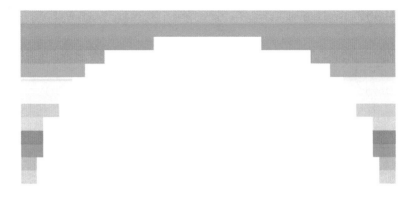

Chapter 1

Geometry in Society

I n society individuals and groups interact and form shapes, operate mechanical motions, transfer, and wield items. The field of social geometry can be carried out in the forming of geometric shapes by people, with their body position, arms, hands, fingers, legs, feet, toes, finger angle, thumb angle, wrist angle, elbow angle, shoulder angle, and a number of biometrical parameters. Postures of the body and gestures with hands, arms, feet, and legs can assist in the formation of geometric shapes.

A group shape is a shape composed by a group of people. A group in a line, at interval of 6 feet between each person is a group shape. A group in a conical formation, with one person standing on a platform that is 10 feet above the surrounding plane, and six people in hexagonal position, where each of the six are at an equal distance to the center and where there is an equal distance between each of the six to the adjacent members is a group shape. This is geometry in a social environment.

In choreography dancers and groups of dancers move and dance in formations, often maintaining a constant distance between corresponding limbs and points on limbs. Bands with musical instruments, formations, and dancers that transit on courses can form geometric shapes.

On streets, sidewalks, and town squares people walk, talk, and carry out business with each other. Geometric forms might emerge between people, such as maintenance of a constant distance between two lines of people, even if the lines are curved. A rotational region might begin to form and continue in a gathering for a period. Movement can start in two parallel lines, one on the left and one on the right, in direction that is 180° angle from each other.

There are geometric shapes in groups of people that form in culture. Distance, number, size, and configurations are a part of social environs. Physical distance is the keeping of certain distances between people for various activities and at times. In a game model, a group might alternate between 4 feet distance from each other to 8 feet distance from each other at an interval of 2 hours for 10 hours. In another model, the members of three groups maintain a distance to the members of the other two groups for a period of 8 hours. Group A keeps 5 feet from group B and 8 feet from Group C. Group B keeps a minimum of 4 feet from Group A and a maximum of 12 feet from Group C. Group C keeps 7 feet from Group A and 9 feet from Group B.

In a group on a search, the formation of people is sometimes one row in width that progresses forward through a region. At a store or venue a line of people might form with one column. Rows and columns are in many group positional arrangements, such as in a choir, in bands with instruments on a field, and tennis with doubles, where two teams of two people play on either side of the net.

The geometric shapes of circles, pyramids, lines, and triangles occur in groups. People gather in circle and arc formations. The direction they point in is a factor. In a bandwagon formation the group points outward of a circle, in the direction of a line from a center point. People sometimes align their direction towards each other in pairs and in gatherings in a one half circle toward a speaker.

There are social phenomenon such as layering, where there are multiple rows of people in a group. Another social phenomenon is circling or looping, where a group forms a closed layer of people with an area interior to the group. Groups that stand in a line and then move from the line for other people to transit through form what may be a conduit.

Geometric shapes can be performed by individuals. Miming is description with gesture and movement. A person who mimes might form shapes with their hands and body to communicate. A person can utilize their arms, hands and fingers to form the vertices, edges, and facets of objects.

There is a geometry in gestures. A person might point with the arm to tell another the direction of a place or event. They may rotate the arm in an arc gesture, horizontal from left to right. The fingers and hands can be utilized to count by raising fingers in sequences. Two fingers can be put at an exact angle for measurements.

Complementary geometric configuration can be formed with impression and continuation of shape. A person holds two arms vertically at 90° elbow angle. The person walks forward and impresses their arms on an object. The arms are conformed to the object, which in turn forms a complementary shape. The shape is continued on to another object, where the arms are impressed on the object to form a shape that is maintained for a period. This is formation of complementary shape and continuation of the configuration of hands.

The postures and shapes formed by an individual or group can be examined in sequence and time. The distance between the thumb and index finger on the right hand every 10 second for 3 years is a biological measurement. The memory of posture of a person may be the posture of the person at a time and date.

Function and procedure can be carried out with the forming of shapes. A man puts his left index finger under his left nostril, then increases the distance of the finger to the nostril. He then puts his right index finger under his right nostril, then increases the distance of the finger to the nostril. The man puts both index fingers on both of the nostrils, left finger to left nostril and right finger to right nostril, and then increases the distance of the fingers to the nostrils. He then does not put a finger on either of the nostrils. The olfactory sense of smell in conjunction with the gesture is a functionality.

Group of People in Shape

A group of people interact with arms straight and at 120°
arc to form a complementary shape. Arms are put parallel
to each other from elbow to wrist. The elbow angles,
parallel positions of the arms, and distance between the
arms are utilized to form the shape in the group.

Group Arranges into Shape

Men and women arrange a shape with their arms that is either straight or at right angle. There are two intersections where three people put their arms into a configuration, one on the left and one on the right. The two men in the center form an intersection of two.

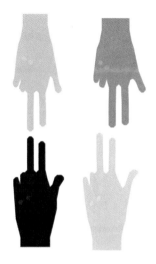

Array and Connection

A group of people put their hands into a 2 x 2 array with the middle and index finger extended. In the first column each of the two extended fingers are corresponding. In the second column, the hand in the first row of the second column has the middle finger corresponding to the index finger of the hand in the second row of the second column. This is a computation with fingers in correspondence.

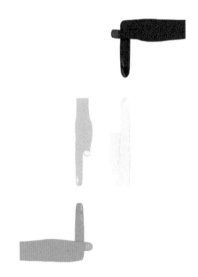

Group with Hands in Arrangement

Four people put their hands into an arrangement. The hands are either straight or at 90° angle at the base knuckles. The four hands are each aligned in a direction. The distance between the tips of the fingers of each hand, where the fingers are aligned towards each other, is equal in length. The arrangement is in a rotational symmetry.

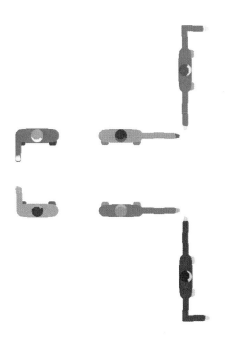

Group Shape A

A group of people form a group shape with their arms. Their arms are either straight, at right angle and aligned to the forward direction, or at right angle and aligned to the up direction. The group forms a group shape with a passage on the left which opens to a section on the right.

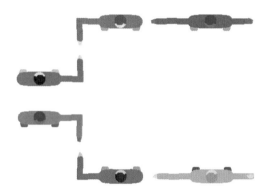

Group Shape B

People form a group shape with their arms. The people form six edges with mirror symmetry to each other. They form edges that are parallel on their arms and on the line from shoulder to shoulder. The length of distance between the lines of people increases to the right.

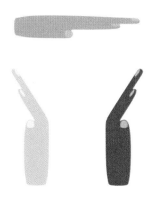

Group in Convergence of Hands A

A group of three people put their hands into a convergence in an equilateral triangle. The hands form line segments of the edges of the triangle, where the hands are either straight or at 120° angle. The hands are aligned vertically with thumb up. Three hand shapes are in spatial alignment.

Group in Convergence of Hands B

Four people put hands into a convergence with two hands along a line and two hands perpendicular. The base knuckle angles and some of the middle knuckle angles are at 120°. This is an interaction of four hand shapes in alignment.

Complementary Shapes

Groups of people are in one of two group shapes. There are five groups. The groups can move to where they are adjacent to form complementary surfaces on edges. The formations are maintained in their shape via rotation, translation, and operations.

Group Arrangement of Hands

A group of people arrange their hands at 90° angle into a geometric shape. The hands are at right angle with the fingers and arms pointed horizontal or vertical. The group shape is three-dimensional with multiple rows and columns.

Discs on Poles

A man is walking amongst vertical stacks of discs on rods. The discs are of various diameters and at different elevations and distances between the discs. The discs and poles are spread apart such that he can walk upright between the stacks.

Man and Woman in Terrain

A man and woman are traversing a terrain that has radial structures of cylinders, rods, and arcs. The cylinders are of various heights and diameters. The arcs are connected via horizontal rods and are symmetrical in rotation at 180° around the poles.

People Form Hand Patterns

People put their hands in four rows and two columns. The distance between each hand in the rows is equal. Each row has two hands that are either straight, diagonal, or at 90° base knuckle angle. A pattern of 2 x 2 hands is formed along the columns.

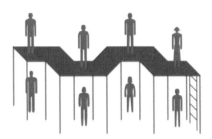

Vertical Array of People

A group is in a vertical array with two rows and four columns in a structure with platforms and a ladder. The array they form with their position has folds on its width, with part of the structure to the forward and part to the back. There can be multiple storey communication with the structure.

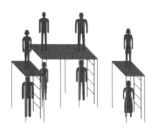

Array and Platforms

Six people are arranged with a structure that has three sets of platforms and ladders with two rows and four columns. An array is formed and curved in a wide arc of an ellipse with sides to the forward and central area to the back.

Group Forms Passage and Channel A

A group forms a bilayer passage and a channel that can facilitate transport. The members of the group are aligned toward the right or the left on either side of the channel. Items can be transferred across the channel from one region to the other and along the middle of the passage.

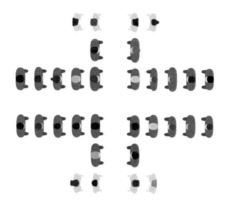

Group Forms Passage and Channel B

A group forms a channel with a passage. The members in the channel form flanges at the entrances of the passage with columns that extend in width. The group can filter items that cross into the channel and through the passage.

Geometric Blocks

Blocks of geometric shapes are strapped to a man at his arms and legs with arm bands and thigh bands. The shape and size of the blocks and the strap position increase or decrease distance in flow of walking or moving on a street or walkway with other people.

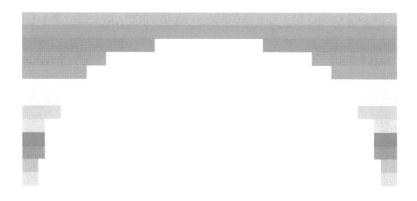

Chapter 2

Mechanics of Groups

In gatherings there might be groups that form shapes, both individually and together. Mechanical motion is another behavior of groups. People can operate motions with hands, arms, feet, legs, rotation of body, angles of feet, knee, waist, and body parts with parameters.

A behavior in which there is mechanical motion is congregation waving. In stadiums the people in the stands raise their hands in waves. When someone within a designated distance raises their arms, they raise their arms. The waves some times come in multiple coruscations.

Directional alignment occurs in gatherings, where if one person rotates to point in a direction, then sometimes others will rotate to point in that direction. At speeches and gatherings when a person is talking people may rotate to align in the direction of the speaker. The people in attendance might form a one half circle, arc, or fan formation with arc rows. Each time a speaker talks the members may rotate toward the new speaker.

The flow of pedestrians walking can be in one direction, or an interaction at two or more directions. The speed of people walking might be different in one area to another. Stationary groups might interact with transiting pedestrians.

In a city block of streets in a grid section, pedestrians can walk in squares around one block, in a figure eight within two blocks, in geometric shapes such as a triangular step, and in concert at a time or on the occurrence of criteria.

Complementary shapes might be formed by groups. Two lines of people can be complementary in shape. A group forms into two columns of people. In each row the people are at equal distance to each other. The distance between rows may or may not be equal. Complementary shapes are formed with postures and gestures. If someone puts their arm into a diagonal gesture, then another person may form the gesture in that direction.

Computation can be conducted with a group. In a formation a group might alternate between two or more shapes or carry out a sequence of motions. Counting with fingers and hands is a computation and an expression of number and geometry. One method of counting is raising the thumb and then the four fingers from index finger to little finger by curling the thumb and fingers in sequence.

A computation between two people may be where they point towards each other, then one rotates 90° to the right and the other stays pointed to the forward. The first person returns in rotation to the forward. The second person rotates 90° to their right and the other stays pointed forward. The second person then rotates to the forward.

Another instance of groups in rotation is a 5 x 5 group of people in an array. They point in a direction and rotate a certain number of degrees clockwise or counterclockwise per minute for 1 hour.

Tools can be utilized in mechanics such as rod, plate, cubical block, and ropes. Members can then operate the tools in their motions. A task can be carried out by the group in their environment.

In relay races runners transfer a relay baton between each other. The relay baton is a rod with air interior. Transference of a baton from one person to another on a course is mechanical motion with a tool in a formation.

Another tool is a disc-shaped sheet held by members around the perimeter of the sheet. The members increase and decrease the elevation of the sheet at different positions on the sheet.

A rope that is tied on a line of people, where each person has a ring, hook, or attachment on the line, is worn on expeditions and in sports, such as spelunking, climbing, and tethering.

A line of people forms a group geometry. There is the distance between adjacent members, the direction that people are pointed, bifurcation of lines, loops internal to a line, and features.

In interaction there are often several elevations in the environ to stand on. Three-dimensional interaction can happen in one or more storey on a structure, across to structures, and between two or more people.

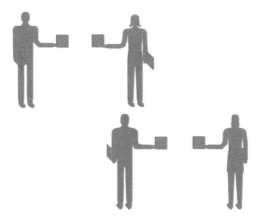

Figures Holding Boards

An array of figures is in a square arrangement. Each of the figures is holding two boards, one to the forward and one perpendicular to the left or right. The boards are in sets of two that correspond to each other over a distance. The direction and positions of the boards are a configuration of the eight boards.

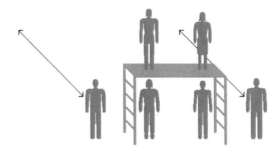

Group with Ladders

A group of people are in a group shape with platforms and ladders. The group alternates between two group shapes. Two of the members transit forward and return on tracks. This is a three-dimensional formation with shape and mechanics conducted by the group.

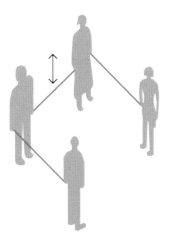

Rod Forms in Alternating Sequence

People in a 2 x 2 formation are holding rods. The group conducts a mechanical motion of moving the elevation of an object. Two of the rods are kept at waist level. The third rod is increased and decreased in elevation in an alternating sequence.

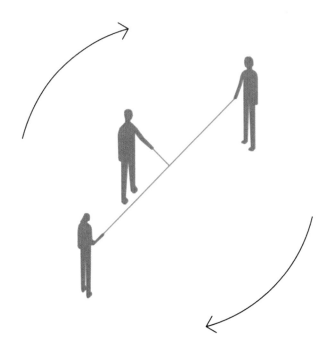

Group Rotation

A group of people hold a bar structure and rotate clockwise. The man and woman holding the long segments traverse a circle that is increased in radius to the circle traversed by the man holding the perpendicular bar. The object is held and utilized by a group.

Groups in Formation

Ten thousand people in a city carry out a group formation in which they put their right arm forward and left arm to the left for 10 minutes at a date and time. The group forms a shape. The postures are formed in any of the directions in which the people may be aligned. The position of the people is not set prior to the formation.

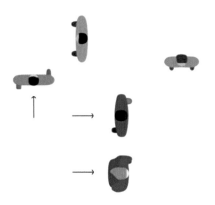

Group and Motion

Five thousand people in a city walk perpendicular to the right 1 per hour for 10 hours at a date and time. The group carries out the motion at a time in which the position and direction of the people are not arranged prior to the group moving.

Line of People at Ten Feet Interval

A line of people is at 10 feet interval to each adjacent person in the line. The line can be set to any number of people. It may curve, rotate angle, and extend in a number of directions. There is a front and back of the line. The direction of orientation of the people is not set in the line.

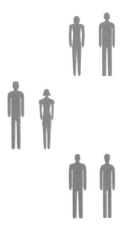

Bifurcating Line of People

A line with people bifurcates into two lines of people. The people can walk along the lines, transport items, and relay information. There are three line segments formed, one segment that branches to two segments. There is one front of the line and two backs to the line.

Square Structures Between Arms

Square structures are held by a group of people between their arms, in the area from the elbow to wrist. The group can maintain an exact distance between their arms at positions with the squares. The objects are utilized for interconnection.

Trapezoid Structures Between Arms

Trapezoidal structures are between the arms of a group of people. The structures are connected together in groups of two. The people put their arms straight and at 90° angle. The structure is held by the people on edges and vertices.

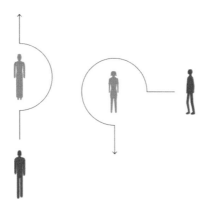

Revolving Games

Groups of people are in a game of revolving. In the game one group walk toward and around, on an arc of 180°, people of a second group at a radius of 4 feet. The second group walks toward and around the members of the other group on an arc of 270° at a radius of 4 feet.

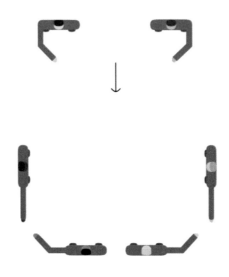

Groups in Formation A

A group of people in a group shape traverse to and arrange a complementary formation with another group. The groups form edges with their arms. They extend their arms straight and at 120° elbow angle to form the complementary shape.

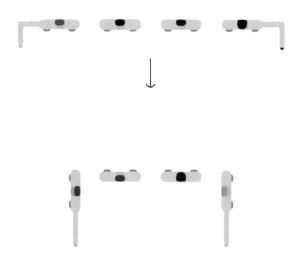

Groups in Formation B

A group of people translate to another group to intercalate and form a complement. One group is in convex postures and the other group is in concave postures. The straight edges are formed with shoulder to shoulder in parallel. The members of one of the groups are aligned in one direction. The members of the other group are aligned in three directions.

Ropes and Rotation A

Ropes are equipped by a group of people. The ropes are connected between their belts. There are ropes in triangular and linear arrangements between the people which can be utilized to rotate and translate. The length of three of the ropes are equal and the fourth rope has a decreased length.

Ropes and Rotation B

A group of people has ropes in between each other. The network of ropes has one triangular arrangement and two linear arrangements. The members in the triangular rope section can rotate as a group and maintain a taut network. The members at the tips of the linear ropes can rotate individually.

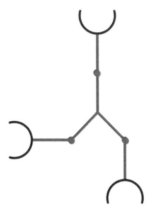

Arm Holders

Three arm holders are a part of a structure with bars at 120° angle. People can put the holders on and arrange into conformations. This is a tool to utilize between people bodily with contact and attachment. The tool is for three people to operate.

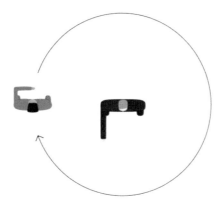

Track and Gestures

A woman walks on a circular track around a man. She keeps a 5 feet distance between him and her as she revolves. The woman has a gesture of left arm at right angle with the elbow to hand tangential to the torso. The man has right arm forward and straight.

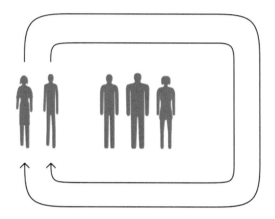

Rows of People

A row of two people walk in a track around another row of three people. The row of two people is perpendicular to the direction of the track on which they traverse. The two people on the track maintain a distance of 2 feet from each other. There is a 5 foot distance between the inner track and the row of three people.

Planks and Rods Between People

Planks are on the head of a man and head of a woman. There are three segments of the structure that can rotate to each other, the two planks with rods and a central rod. The central rod is connected with hinges to the planks and rods at either tip.

Sets of Rods

Three sets of rods are in between the arms of two people, from the elbow to the wrist. The man and woman utilize pressure to hold the rods. The distance between rods is proximate and distant. The pattern is proximate, distant, distant, and then proximate.

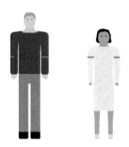

Rods on Armbands

People are wearing rods on armbands. There is a rod on
the left arm and three rods on the right arm of the two
people. They can adjoin rods in parallel and perpendicular
arrangements. The rods on armbands are clothing
accessories that can be utilized to interact bodily in a
group.

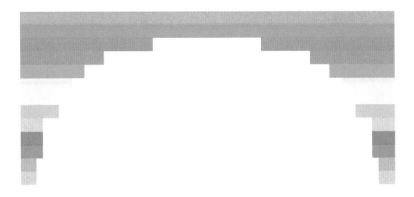

Chapter 3

Audio and Video Landscapes

Soundscape ecology is the study of the acoustic sounds in the environment generated from biological species and the geological and physical phenomenon in the area and how species interact with each other via sound.

Anthrophony is the sounds that humans make in an environment. This may be speech, humming, and the engine noise of machinery. Biophony is the sounds emitted by biological species, such as the rustle of leaves in trees, water splashing from fish, and the sound of hoofs in herding species. Geophony is physical and geological sounds. This can be rain, rocks tumbling on a slope of a hill, and waves coming ashore at a beach.

An array of speakers has a 10 x 10 grid of cells, where there is a speaker in each cell and a recorded sound that is emitted by the speaker when the speaker is selected. The speakers in the grid will emit the sounds in spatial relation in an array of a sound description. If there is a sound of an object at that position in the area, then the speaker may emit a sound of that object. If there is a door at that position, then the sound of a door moving on hinges might be emitted. If there is a vase at a position in the grid, then the sound of water pouring might be emitted when the speaker is activated. This is a soundscape. A region, object, or abstract idea can be transmitted with an array of sounds.

Auditory and visual corresponds to audio and video. A landscape of audio and video devices is an interaction zone to navigate and communicate in. A landscape of audio can be phones, speakers, beepers, and alarms for recording and transmitting sound. A video landscape can be video recorders to record and screens to transmit visual content.

Multiple devices can be put in arrays and arranged over a broad area. The devices can be set individually or orchestrated to move on tracks of a number of lengths and directions. There can be a distribution of devices in networks to explore.

The audio devices do not need to be electronic. Strings and pipes can transmit sound in networks. A number of instruments can emit sounds of specific pitch, amplitude, direction, timing, and qualities.

Video recorders may record visual phenomena. Video recorders might be stationary or move. They can move along tracks on railings, rotate at a constant speed in gears, remain fixed to objects which might move, or be in a number of states of motion.

Screens emit an output of an array of light to describe a visual input. A screen can be of many sizes, two-dimensional or curved. There are triangular or elliptic shaped screens.

Visual output can emanate from devices that are not screens, such as strings of lights, lightbulb bars, and laser light. Blinkers flash light at regular intervals. Rotating lightbulbs with walls on sides convey light in patterns. There are reflectors that might be stationary or rotate.

Multiple devices can be set in an environment, in geometric formations or dispersed, that gather input and emit an output. The device may be at a mesoscale that can be walked in and navigated through.

There are devices that two or more people may operate. String telephony is two cups with an opening at the base of the cups and a string that connects between the two openings. One person puts a cup to their ear and a second person speaks into the second cup, then the speaker puts the cup to their ear and the other person speaks into the first cup.

An audio or video device can be translated, rotated, or transformed in a geometric or kinetic manner. A string that is vibrating on its length can be rotated, revolved, and moved in a straight line. When the bell of a clarinet is lifted and then moved beneath the mouthpiece this is a motion of the instrument that is a part of the sound that is emitted by the clarinetist.

An open system receives input and materials into its system. Closed systems don't allow input and passage of materials in or out of the system. The carriage and transmittance of sound is essential for an open system. Sounds from regions are recorded, transported, and emitted in other regions.

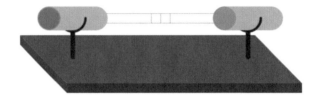

String Telephone with Net

A string telephone has two cups with a taut string between the base of the cups via holes. Sound in a cup is transmitted from the cup, along the string and into the other cup. Above is a string telephone with a net of two strings.

Pipes to Set to Ear

There is a network of pipes on a pedestal that people may set their ears to. To the left three pipes are in a fixed 120° angle. To the right is a pipe with 180° angle. The pipes are connected along the central pipe. The two sets of pipes can be rotated.

Corridor

A man stands in front of a corridor of plates, where two ridges decrease in height to a basin. There are ledges on the ridges and basin. The plates are corrugated to the right. Sound can be transmitted in air, pipes of a speaker, and in a basin.

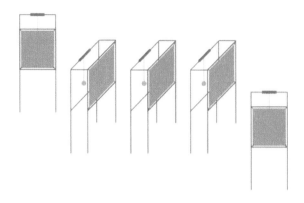

Track of Gongs

A track with gongs at interval along its length has motorized mallets that percuss on the gongs at algorithm. Gongs can percuss along a sequence and cascade. This set of gongs turns in direction two times on its course. Each gong is within 8 feet of the adjacent gong or gongs.

Speaker Circuit on Blocks

Speakers are on a circuit that has blocks of three elevations. The speakers translate in grooves on linear tracks to any position on the tracks. One of the tracks is perpendicular to three of the tracks. A sound or multiple sounds can be emitted from one to four of the speakers.

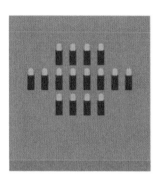

Array of Speakers A

An array of speakers transmits sound in a geometric shape of rows and columns. The array is symmetrical and not rectangular. Not all cells in rows are with a corresponding column of one or more cells and not all cells in columns are with a corresponding row of one or more cells.

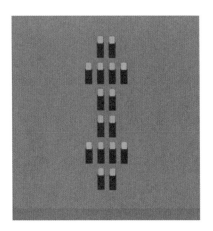

Array of Speakers B

Speakers in an array are in six rows and four columns. The distance between adjacent vertical and adjacent horizontal speakers is one centimeter. One or more of the speakers can emit sound at a time. The array is a sound corridor.

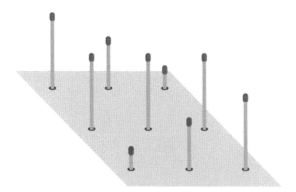

Array of Speakers that Elevate

A 3 x 3 array of speakers increase and decrease in elevation on poles. The distance between each adjacent speaker in rows and columns is 5 feet. The poles of the speakers are 6 feet in height and can vary in the range of 0-6 feet.

Volume Landscape

Speakers in a 3 x 3 array are on a board that is 2.5 centimeters². Each speaker is 1 centimeter from adjacent speakers in each row and column. The device measures the volume of sound at a time in the area of the array. Nine decibels values are recorded. The sounds with corresponding amplitudes are emitted as a description of sound in an environ.

Speaker with Crank

A speaker on a pedestal can be rotated via a crank. A speaker can translate, rotate, and move in a number of kinds of motion. The speaker can be rotated clockwise and counterclockwise any number of degrees with a period of not being rotated.

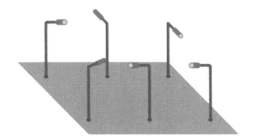

Cameras in Array

Photography is presented with direction in an area. A 3 x 2 array of cameras are on poles. The cameras can rotate 360°. The distance between the poles of the adjacent cameras on rows and columns is 6 feet. The cameras photograph in algorithmic sequences to time, number, and angle of camera.

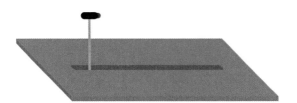

Video Recorder on Track

A video recorder is on a linear track. The video recorder moves forward and back with the video recorder aligned toward the right. The video recorder operates according to algorithm, such as the video recorder moving forward 1 per minute for 10 seconds, then moving back. The video recorder is 6 feet in height.

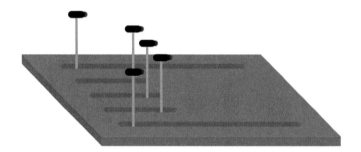

Video Recorders on Rows of Tracks

Video recorders move along rows of five tracks at equal intervals. The grooves of the tracks are of different lengths. The video recorders are programed to start at positions, move at designated speeds, and remain at positions for a time.

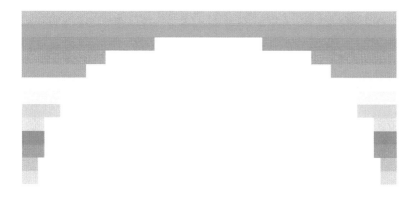

Chapter 4

Sight & Hearing

The five senses are sight, hearing, smell, touch, and taste. The sense of sight is vision and the organs of sight are the eyes. The sense of hearing is audition and the organs of hearing are the ears. The sense of smell is olfaction and the organ of smelling is the nose. The sense of touch is tactile and the organ of touch is the skin. The sense of taste is gustation and the organ of taste is the tongue.

There are further senses, such as magnetoreception, the sense of magnetic North and magnetic motion, thermoreception, the sense of heat, equilibrioception, the sense of balance, and pressure sense.

The sense of sight pertains to the eyes, electromagnetic radiation, and descriptions of what is seen. Qualia are instances of experience. The sensation of color, the pitch of a sound, and the warmth of hot blowing air are qualia. Qualia of sight might be silhouettes on a wall, rotating light in a beacon, and beams of hues in a prism. Hue, value, shade, and intensity are qualities of sight.

Clothing accessories, handheld items, and structures can be utilized for examination of sight. Telescopes can magnify distant objects and microscopes magnify microscopic objects. Stained glass panes in windows put a translucent hue between the observer and the area to view.

The sense of hearing pertains to ears, compression waves in air, and descriptions of what is heard. Qualia of hearing might be echoes in a canyon, the Doppler Effect of a sound emitter moving by, or the sound of a thrust underwater. Frequency, amplitude, pitch, tone, and timbre are qualities of sound.

Hearing can be examined with accessories to wear, items to hold, and structure to interact with. Geological landforms such as canyons and cliffs relay echoes. Speaking into blowing air or a fan increases and decreases amplitude of sound. Attachments to the ear set with ear hooks or held by headbands can generate sound phenomena.

Sound is transmitted as compression waves in air. Sound can be transmitted through water and other liquids as compression waves. The sound of splashing, vertical oscillation of a hull, and motion through water sometimes traverse through water.

There are social interactions with two or more people that pertain to sight and hearing. On sight there is a gestural game. A person gestures to another person. The second person then presents the gesture to a third person. The third person gestures what they saw to a fourth person, in a line from one to another.

On hearing there is the telephone game. In the game there is a line of people. The first person speaks a sentence to the second person in line. The second person speaks the sentence they heard to the third person in the line. From person to person the people convey what they heard. The sound is transmitted along a geometric formation in a sequence by the group. The words, the number of words, and the order of the words are to be spoken so that they are correct and not partial or repeating.

Headband with Holders for Photographs

On a headband with four pads there are eight slot holders for photographs. The photographs are inserted into the slots towards the person wearing the headband. The slots can hold papers with text, numbers, shapes, and drawings.

Openings that can Rotate

A woman is standing at a structure that has two square openings on a pedestal. The openings can rotate their angle between each other. The openings are at the height of the eyes. There are visual vantages with the openings at different angles.

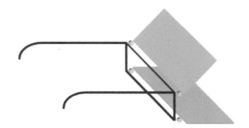

Headband and Panels

A headband has two panels on a rectangular structure. The angle of the panels can be between 90° and 270°, where 0° is to the forward of the headband. The panels can increase, decrease, and hold stationary in angle. This structure may be set to present a viewing area.

Viewing Platform A

There is a viewing platform that is a tube that maintains the height of the tube, then increases the height to the right. The viewing window is the rectangular opening at the left which expands to the opening at the right. A line of sight is through the window.

Viewing Platform B

There is a viewing platform that is a tube that has a section that decreases in height. The viewing window is from the left opening to the right opening. The area in the tube has concave and convex surfaces. Line of sight can occur between the left and right rectangular openings.

Perimeter Plate on Ear Hook

A perimeter plate on an ear hook has an opening of a symmetrical shape. The plate is put around the ear and extends outward. The plate is a tube with a surface that maintains its shape in cross section along the course of the tube.

Ear Attachment with Pulley and Perforation

An ear attachment with an ear hook has a pulley attached with perforation along a strip. The pulley can be operated to put sections of the perforated strip at the ear. The perforation has either an opening or not an opening per cell on one column.

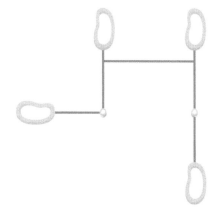

Network of Perimeter Plates to Put to Ear

A network of perimeter plates to put to ear are connected with a structure. The plates are in the shape of an ear. Two of the plates are connected in fixed position to the structure. The remaining plates are on rotational rods. A group of people can arrange into configurations with the plates.

Instrument with Letter Pipes

A pipe that is a musical instrument has a mouthpiece to blow on. Along the length of the pipe are openings to which pipes can be inserted in the shape of letters. There may or may not be one or more openings in the letter pipes.

Instrument with Pipes of Geometric Shapes

Pipes of geometric shapes are attached to a linear pipe with openings. The openings are either disc-shaped or are arced in shape. The pipes may be linear, branched, diverge and then converge, or expand and contract on their course.

Soap Bubble Film on Board A

Soap bubble fluid is put on a board with a disc opening. The fluid is applied over the opening in a layer of film. The board is then put to ear. The water, soap, shape of the opening, thickness of the film, and distance to the ear effects the transmission of sound. This is a liquid medium for terrestrial navigation.

Soap Bubble Film on Board B

The motion of sound through water is hydroacoustics. A board with an elliptic opening is put to ear. The board has soap bubble film applied to the opening. The speed, pitch, and amplitude of sound is increased in water. The speed of sound is increased with an increase in temperature.

Structure with Tubes

A structure to wear is set to ear via an opening. The structure has two vertical tubes with disc openings and a tube with a rectangular opening to the forward. This is a tube that trifurcates into three tubes from one tube. The three tubes vary in diameter over their length.

Cross Tube Network

Two cross tubes are connected via a linear tube. The cross tubes are perpendicular. On two tubes of each of the cross tubes there is an opening shaped in the perimeter of the ear. A person can put the tubes to ear. The remaining tubes are disc openings.

Branching Pipes

A pipe that bifurcates into two pipes is on a rod and holder. The ear is set to the single tube on the left. Sounds in the area will transmit through one or both of the pipes on the right and then converge to the pipe on the left or transmit through one or both pipes on the right.

Pipe Branch Networks

A woman wears a network of pipes that are over each of her ears. The pipes bifurcate into two pipes and then converge to one pipe. Sound transmitting through the pipes transmit to one or both pipes, diverge, and then converge.

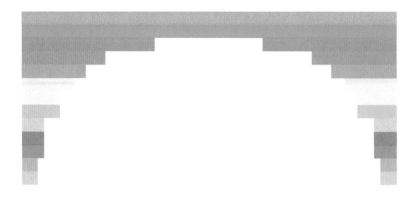

Chapter 5

Smell & Touch

Olfactics is the study of the the sense of smell and the scents that are experienced. An odorant is a substance that spreads a smell. Odorants might be minerals, liquids, or plant material. Sulfur, chalk, and clay are mineral odorants. Water, oil, and acetone are liquid odorants. Leaves, bark, needles, cones, petals, herbs, and spices are plant material odorants.

There are many smells, such as sweet, floral, woody, resinous, minty, spicy, fruity, nutty, lemon, pungent, ethereal, and camphoraceous. The smell of cleaning chemicals is ethereal. The smell of camphor is camphoraceous. Odorants with camphor are sage and rosemary.

Blowing, tumbling, heating, and chipping materials disperses chemicals and generates scents. Odorants might be dispersed by mechanical motions, mixing, and chemical reactions. Odorants may be arrayed in structures that can hold solids, liquids, and gases, in two and three dimensions. Odorant dispersal might be opened or closed by rubbing to release gases or opened with valves.

Instruments and items worn can arrange odorants. A nose attachment with elliptical openings for the nostrils alters air pressure coming in and out of the nose. Four openings in a row on a plate can be a four-nostril attachment. The gaseous content flows through four openings and then to the nostrils of the nose.

The science of touch is the study of the sense of touch and feelings of contact. A touchant is that which is touching or moving at the skin. Touchants might be the wind, a cloth wrist sleeve, or a chair. Porous rocks, rubber, and steel are touchant solids. H_2O, alcohol, and gasoline are liquid touchants. Blowing air, balloon pressure, and bubbles of carbonation in water are gaseous touchants.

Qualia of touch can be traction that is tangential to the body, gas pressure, water pressure, and evaporation of water on the skin. Qualities of touch are pressure, vibration, smooth, and rough.

Touch can be conducted with clothing and patterning. One day I put an array of raised dots on the interior of the back of the front of a shirt. The array I put to the top section of the shirt. The pattern of dots I set to the Fibonacci Sequence of 1, 1, 2, 3, 5, continuing indefinitely. The sequence was in an array with rows and columns, from left to right and top to bottom. The texture on the inside of a cloth can be arranged to convey a tactile environment.

Touch can be applied with water. In perspiration, water will gather on the surface of the body, evaporate in a breeze or wind, and cool the person. Shapes may be traced in water onto the body. The water is then blown with a fan. The water evaporates and cools the skin.

Containers of Potpourri that Rotate for Nostrils

Two containers on a platform are put to the nostrils of the nose. Potpourri is set into the containers. The containers are in angular segmentation and can rotate. Potpourri is put into all, some, or none of the segments. The containers can be stationary or rotate a certain number of degrees.

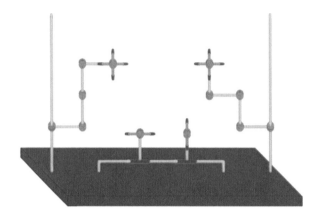

Rods and Hinges with Substances to Smell

A network of rods are on a board. There are two poles on which rods translate vertically and rotate on hinges. A rod with a horizontal section has tubes that translate horizontally. Rods that rotate are connected to the tubes. Substances are layered on the rods to smell.

Nose Attachment with Ring of Containers of Potpourri

Attached to a holder for the nose is a ring of containers connected via a rod. There are sixteen containers on the interior of the ring in a single row cell formation in a loop. Potpourri is put into the containers. Each cell has potpourri or not potpourri.

Container of Potpourri

A container in the shape of a dodecahedron, one of the five Platonic Solids, has twelve holders for potpourri on the twelve facets of the polyhedron. There are twelve up positions on a table and 360° of rotation for each of the positions.

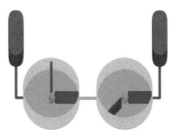

Attachment to Nostrils with Pie Containers

An attachment for the nostrils has two containers with sections to put potpourri. Partitions connected to the central rods of the containers can be rotated to form areas of various sizes. There are two areas that sum in angle to 360° in the containers.

Ring Stack

Ten substances in the shape of rings are stacked in a column. The substances from top to bottom are caramel, butterscotch, brown sugar, mint, cinnamon, chocolate, mint, brown sugar, cinnamon, and chocolate. The substance is put to the nose and smelled. The aromas waft through the central tube.

Stacks of Substances

An attachment for the nostrils has two columns of containers to put beneath the nose with a column beneath each nostril. The containers can hold substances to smell. An opening is in the center of each container. Scents expand up the stacks through the openings and around the sides.

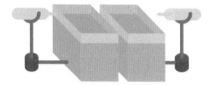

Air Sprayers and Containers

Two containers are on blocks that can be put beneath the nostrils. Air sprayers are held at each container to spray substances put in the containers. The speed of the sprayers can be increased and decreased, turned on and off, and alternate from left to right.

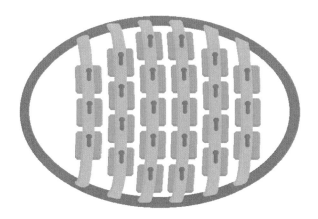

Headband with Pads

A headband has six arc bars on which are pads. The pads can be moved vertically on rods. The pads exert a tactile press onto the head. Configurations of pads press in sequences to communicate. A tactile event can be recorded and pressed to tell a story with touch.

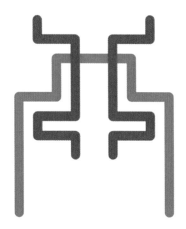

Tracks of Water on Body

Three sets of tracks of water are put onto the body. The blue track has a temperature of 18.2° C. The two red tracks are at a temperature of 41.6° C. This is an evaporation track with temperature variation. The blue track is traced first, then the left and right red tracks are traced.

Instrument to Press on Body

An instrument on a handle has ten rods to press on the body. The rods can translate on the bar through loops at their base. The distance between rods can be set and pressed. The interval between rods is set to one centimeter.

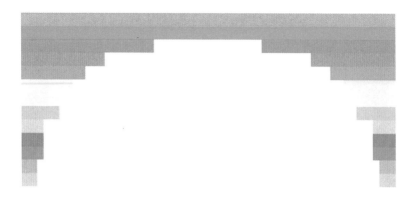

Chapter 6

Taste, Magnetoreception, and Senses

The fifth sense of the five senses is taste. The science of taste is the study of the sense of taste and the tastants that are felt. Gustation is the sense of taste. Salt, sugar, caramel, and water are tastants. Qualia of taste can be hot food, powder, paste, and liquid. Qualities of taste are sweet, salty, sour, bitter, and umami.

The field of food science is the study of food synthesis, preparation, and preservation. Culinary arts is the preparation and presentation of food. The food, utensils, dinnerware, heaters, and items are utilized in the presentations of food.

In tasting, substances can be evaluated as to whether to ingest, drink, or inhale. A person can heat food, move food, particularize substances to sense an increased surface area, and arrange conduction and convection between the tongue and the food.

The arrangement of food is a part of food science. A plate with holes is filled with food and put on the tongue. The food is pressed into the shapes of the holes. Each hole can be filled with one or more kinds of food. The shape, size, depth, and distribution of holes can arrange the type and proportion of food over time.

There are many other senses that might be experienced. Magnetoreception is the sense of magnetic North and of the motions of magnets, metals, and magnetic phenomenon. A magnet on a needle that rotates to north and touches the body is magnetoreception via the skin and tactile sense. Push, pull, and levitation are qualia of magnetoreception.

Thermoreception, the sense of heat, can be somatic. Qualia of thermoreception may be convective heat from a heater and fan, conductive heat of a heater, and liquid heat in water.

Equilibrioception, the sense of balance, pertains to up and down, left and right, and forward and back. The posture of the body, carrying of items, and the distribution of weight are part of balancing. The outward push of centrifugal force and inward push of centripetal force are qualia of equilibrioception.

One day I was on a walk in Buffalo, New York. I filled two vials one half full of water and attached them to my wrists with arm sleeves. The water would generate waves that distributed the weight of the vials. I balanced to the weight as I walked.

Pressure sense is another of the senses. The pressure may be solids, liquids, and gases on the skin. Forward pressure, rotational pressure, water pressure in a region of water, and wind on the skin, are qualia of pressure sense.

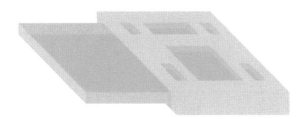

A Circuit of Food with Perforation

A circuit of food has rectangular perforation of different sizes and shapes. A holder for food with panel siding is inserted beneath the perforated top into a slot. The food is tasted by the tongue through the perforation. Food pressed into a cake in the holder would be ingested through six openings. The perforation is a circuit of food.

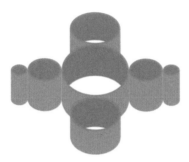

Connected Tubes to Put on Tongue

A group of connected tubes are put on the tongue. Solid, liquid, and gaseous food is ingested through the tubes. There are four diameters of tubes. A food can be applied to all of the tubes or the food items can be put in one or more of the tubes.

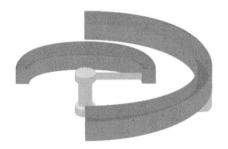

Arc Containers to Put Food

Arc containers that revolve on a rod can be filled with food and put into the mouth. There is an inner and outer container, each of which has an arc length of 180°. This is a manually operated mechanical food tool that is a utensil. The utensil can be configured into many conformations.

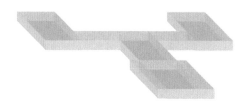

Food Circuit with Containers

An array of containers in two shapes are a food circuit that can be put in the mouth. The containers are a square shape and a rectangular shape. The types, number, and position of attachment are designated for the circuit. The attachment can be at vertex or edge.

Food Containers

Two food containers are connected with a hinge and can rotate. The containers are a food circuit. In this type of food circuit items of food are on lines that can be straight or at angles. The structure is set on the tongue or can be on a tray to taste.

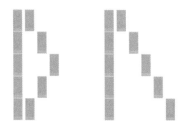

Rows and Columns of Food Containers

Food containers are arranged in rows and columns for two sets. The containers are 5 millimeters x 10 millimeters in size. There are two sets of containers, one on the left and one on the right. In each set are lines of containers that are straight, diagonal, or oscillatory. The distance between food increases or decreases the time for the food to mix.

Magnet with Iron Plates

A magnet is on a bracelet. The bracelet has a bar on which there are iron plates that can rotate. Brushes are connected beneath the plates. A person can wear the bracelet. The iron plates will rotate with the magnet and the brushes will translate on the body.

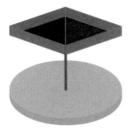

Magnetoreception and Smell

A magnet on a needle that can rotate to north has two containers at top, one on the north section of the magnet and another on the south section of the magnet. The containers can hold substances to smell. Substances are put in the containers. If the magnet rotates, the substances will rotate and this may be detected by smell. The containers on the magnet utilize smell for magnetoreception.

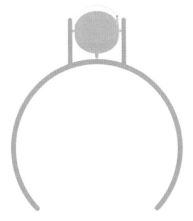

Water Balance in Disc Container

A bracelet has a disc container, where half of the volume of the container is H2O. There is a planar distribution of water for balancing. The disc container can be rotated and has a weight beneath to orient up. Motion of the water in the container puts pressure on the body to balance.

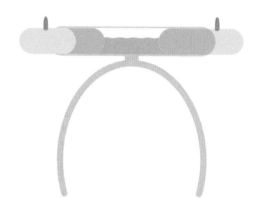

Tube of H_2O and Pistons on Bracelet

A tube of H_2O that has two pistons is on a bracelet. The distribution of weight is based in part on the volume of water, volume of tube, shape of tube, and depth of water. The pistons can translate to increase and decrease the depth of the H_2O.

Tube of Water and Senses

The motion of water is specified by the shape of a container. A tube of water that has two bulbs is in a bracelet. The shape of the tube expands and contracts at the bulbs. The flow of water will increase or decrease as the shape of the tube expands and contracts.

Ring of Water

Equilibrioception is the sense of balance and orientation in space. Accessories to wear can assist in balance. A ring to put on a finger is tubular and filled one half with water. The motion of the water forms waves that alter the distribution of weight.

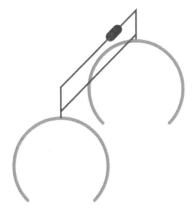

Balance and Weight

A cobalt bead with a hole through the bead can translate along a rod on a bracelet. Balancing when wearing the bracelet is based in part on the element, mass, volume, phase of matter, shape of the element, and length of the rod.

Ring of Iron Balls

Spherical iron balls are in a tubular ring. The ring is an accessory to wear. The balls fill one half of the volume of the interior of the ring. A person can balance in locomotion with iron balls. The mass of iron and the size of the iron balls are parameters in weight distribution.

Bracelet with Bellows

Bellows are attached to a bracelet that is tangential to the arm. The bellows has a motor that compresses the bellows 1 per minute. The air flow from the bellows interacts with the skin. Tactile and olfactory sensations might form in the air currents.

Bracelet and String on Rods

A bracelet has a string that translates vertically on rods. The string vibrates at a distance from the arm in the air above the skin. Particulates in the air interact with the string. The amplitude of the vibration varies with atmospheric conditions, such as wind speed and rain.

Wind Plate on Bracelet

A plate that can rotate in the wind is on a bracelet. The plate is connected to a rod that bifurcates into two rods, where one of the rods has an increased diameter. When the wind blows, the plate might move, which causes the rods to revolve and press on the skin.

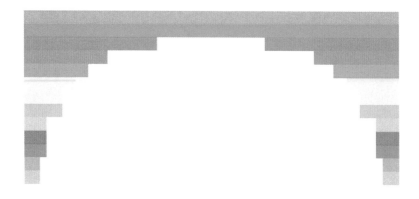

Chapter 7

Locomotion, Interaction, and Biometrics

Locomotion is the movement of an organism with a magnitude and direction from one location to another. Types of locomotion are walking, running, swimming, flying, gliding, undulation, ciliary motion, and saltation, which is hopping with both feet or paws. Humans are bipedal in locomotion, walking and running on two leg limbs.

Ciliary locomotion is swimming and gliding on cilia. Unicellular eukaryotes and a number of animals move in ciliary locomotion. Cilia are vibrating extensions on the surface of cells that can propel an organism forward or move water and materials over cells.

Undulatory locomotion is wave motion conducted with the body to propel the organism forward. In a fish the undulation can be anguilliform, along the whole length of the body, subcarangiform, increasing amplitude of undulation towards the tail, carangiform, oscillation in proximity to the tail, thunniform, undulation at the tail, or ostraciiform, undulation at the tail fin. A human can walk with legs from thigh to feet, knee to feet and ankles to feet. The arm may be rotated at the shoulder, elbow, wrist, base, middle, and top knuckles.

In interaction with people there is the direction of motion of the people in the area, the grouping of people, and the physical distance between people. Terrain and objects in the area must be in account when navigating.

In a concourse, road, or sidewalk there is a maximal width for passage in a walk lane or area to walk through. In a lot, lawn, square, or area to congregate in, people in groups might move when people in other groups move.

Clothing accessories can be equipped and worn that may result in effects to locomotive interaction, in their shape, weight, size, and mechanics. Skis, roller skates, roller blades and stilts are footwear that increase or decrease the speed, traction, and height for the person to interact with.

Travel may occur in the terrestrial environ and in aquatic and cold environs. Swim fins and finger webbing gloves are often worn when swimming in water. Ice skates and snowshoes can be worn when traversing ice.

The mechanics of the linear and angular motion of the body is based on factors such as length and angle of limbs. Biometrics is the measurement of biological parts, mechanics, and processes, along with the statistical analysis of measurement. The measuring of height, weight, and angle of body parts are bodily measurements.

Measurements can be done at one point in time or over a period. The distance between the thumb and index finger over time is a sequence of biometrical data. Measurements can be carried out for individuals and groups of people.

Woman with Board that Rotates on Holders

A woman has a vertical board that rotates on holders on her back. The motion of the board transforms the distribution of weight. The board increases the weight at her back and to the left and right. The board might oscillate laterally as she walks and moves.

Casing Affixed with Rod

In regions of dense population the flow of pedestrians forms moving shapes. In the environment there are buildings and objects to navigate around and through. A man on a walk has a casing affixed with a rod at the waist. The casing is a loop that is elongated to the back. To move through an area the man walks through openings with an increased width to the sides and in rotation.

Band and Rod Held at Belt

A band is held by a rod to the belt on a man. The band is a wide platform around the waist. The band is between two radii from the center of the midline of the body. The center of the ring is open for his arms and legs to move. The band extends the physical distance to navigate with objects in an area and reduces surface area at the waist.

Vertical Torus at Belt

Belts are clothing items that are circumferential at the waist. A torus can be a clothing item that wraps around the body at the middle. A woman has a vertical torus around her belt on a rod. The height of the torus is between her waist and stomach. The torus is at a radius from the midline of the body.

Casing of Boards on Belt

Casing is connected to a man via rods at his belt. Vertical boards on the sides and back are attached to the rods. The casing is at the waist up to the chest. A part of the circumference of the waist has boards between the man and the environment.

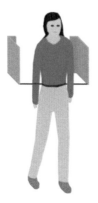

Casing at the Belt

A woman has a casing of vertical boards attached to horizontal rods at her belt. The casing is at the waist to the shoulders and wraps from the left and right to the back. The distance and height of the boards increases horizontal and vertical distances to objects when traveling in a terrain.

A Man with Rotational Rods on Structures

A man is standing with structures attached to his arms via bracelets. Rods of two lengths are attached in alternation to the structures. The rods can remain stationary or rotate. The rotation of the rods toward the midline of the body increase angular velocity.

Panel Structure

On the shoulders at the neck and head of a woman is a structure. The structure is a set of panels in a concavity with an indention for the head. There are two vertical panels to the left and right and a vertical panel of increased height to the back.

Tubes on Arms

A woman has tubes on her arms from the shoulders to the elbows. She can move her arms in the tubes within an area. The range of movement of the arms in the tubes is based on the angle of the arms, the shape of the tubes, and the size of tubes.

Rods at Angle on Arm

Rods that can rotate on a circular measurement ring are on the right arm of a man. The angle of the rods can be set to the angle of the elbow. The extension and flexion of the arm is aligned to the angle of the rods. The ring can be retained at an angle in a state of rotation.

Angular Measurement at Chin

Two rods are on a hinge at the chin. The angle of the rods can be increased and decreased for measurement of the chin angle. The hinged rods can be set to the angle of the body on a part of the body at a concavity, convexity, or linear area.

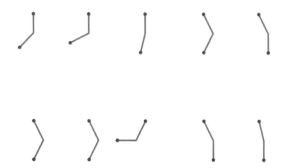

Angle of Right Leg of Ten People

The angle of the knee from the thigh to the knee to the
ankle of the right leg of ten people is measured in degrees
at a time. The angle, position, shape, size, and direction of
the legs form a group shape. This is a biometric state of
the group.

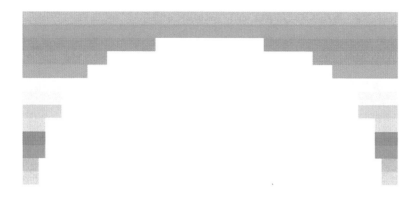

Chapter 8

Language

The presentation of linguistic structures may be carried out with arrays of grids of letters of the Alphabet in linear, two-dimensional, three-dimensional, circular, and concentric shapes. The units in the cells might be letters, concatenated letters, words, and phrases.

Language is conveyed visually with graphemes and in sound with phonemes. Graphemes might be letters, pictograms, and logograms. Olfactory language has smells and odorants that evaporate and sublimate substances to smell in structures to present in language.

Braille is a tactile language with raised dots in cells. The cells are arrays of three rows and two columns, where there can be a raised dot or not a raised dot for each position in the array. To each cell there is a corresponding letter, number, operator, or punctuation mark.

On the matter of taste and language, plates can be covered with edible substance in the shape of letter fonts on a plate or there can be indentions in the shape of letters of the Alphabet in the plate to put food to be tasted. Icing can be written in the shape of letters on cakes with icing extruders.

Language can be linear, two-dimensional, and pyramidal. Physical structures can be arranged to build lettering and sentence composition with translation, cycles, rotation, and geometric transformations on mechanical constructs.

Olfactory language can be presented with letters of the Alphabet. Pictograms, logograms, and geometric shapes can be utilized for olfactory conveyance. One or more substances to smell may be put in adjacent, layered, or concentric format.

Computation is analog, digital, quantum, or another kind of computing. Computations may be discrete and binary, 1 and 0, or multidirectional and continuous with more than two inputs and / or outputs.

In digital computing 1 and 0 are increased voltage and decreased voltage. In analog computing structures can translate and rotate to designated markings. Slide rules and radial dials are analog computers.

An analog computer has a physical quantity as a variable on a continuous range. A dial that can point in 360° has a direction. The direction is a variable on a ring for the physical dial needle. Computation can be carried out with many physical structures and processes.

3D Word with Multiple Direction Pronunciation

A 3D word composed of letters of the Alphabet in a 3D array has multiple directions of pronunciation. The pronunciation can be on the x, y, and z axes. The letters can be pronounced cyclically. Two or more pronunciations of a letter can be uttered. Either all or some of the letters are to be pronounced.

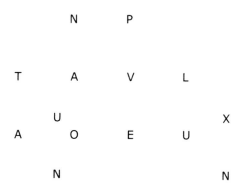

3D Word with Facets

Three facets of letters in an array are in a perpendicular arrangement to adjacent facets. Pronunciation is from adjacent letters that are either vertical, horizontal, or diagonal. The 3D word has letters that are a part of the word if the letters are adjacent to another letter in the word.

Containers in Shape of Letters to Put Potpourri

Containers in the shape of letters of the Alphabet can be filled with potpourri. One of the containers has one layer and the other container is bilayer. The tittle, which is a single dot above the non capitalized letters i and j, can be connected with a bar.

Indentions to Put Potpourri in as Olfactory Language

Five tablets with 2 x 3 indentions are in a row. The indentions can be filled with potpourri or a substance that has a scent. This is an olfactory language. Each matrix of indentions can be assigned a letter of the Alphabet. A language might designate that a specific substance be put in an indention or the language may be based on the shape of the indentions. Both substance and shape may be designated.

Layers of Substance to Smell with Indentions

A strip of two layers of substances to smell are on a board. The substances are corn starch and brown sugar from top to bottom. Indentions are put into the strip with a stylus for a language of olfaction. The stylus can be pressed to the depth of one or two layers.

Plates Inscribed with Letters

Plates are connected via hinges with letters inscribed on the plates. The letters can be put in a row of one to three in a line. The letters are in a sequence that can be linear or circular. The plates may be components of letter sequences and words.

Letter Blocks A

Two blocks of letters that are columns of letters connect with a hinge to form letter combinations along the x and y axes. The letter sequence utilized can be the top row, bottom row, both rows, first column, second column, both columns, diagonal, or another sequence.

Letter Blocks B

Two blocks in rows are connected to a structure of rods with tubes to translate and rotate on. A block can form a letter sequence on a row or be moved to another row to generate another sequence on that row. Radial movement can put the sequence in another direction.

Letter Blocks on Track

A track of five rods has blocks inserted of two or three letters of the Alphabet that may translate vertically upon the track. The track is two-dimensional and the letters are in sequences of two and three. The track is a letter and word building structure.

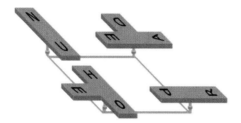

Array of Blocks of Letters

A 2 x 2 array of blocks of letters are on a structure of bars. There are two or three letters, where the letters are in a linear formation or a two-dimensional intersection. A word can be put along two dimensions. One or more lines of letters can be utilized.

Network of Fan Hinges

A 2 x 2 array of hinges are on a structure. The rotating component of the hinges are angular sections at 90°, 120°, 25°, and 45°. The fan sections can come in contact with one or more of the adjacent fans along the arc tip of the fans.

Network of Branching Hinges

A network of hinges connects between boards. The hinges connect two or three boards and form into branches. The two directional hinges can fold or not fold. The three directional hinges can fold at two, one, or none of the edges of the hinge.

Plates in Conformation

A set of plates are connected via hinges on the edges of their facets. There are one to two edges with hinges. The plates can be rotated 360°. This hinge network has three dimensions of rotation. There can be h number of hinges on a plate. A plate network can be triangular, rectangular, and n-gon with increased facets.

Perforation and Pipe on Board

A board has a perforation of an opening and a pipe in a linear sequence. Openings can be in one to multiple dimensions, on a linear section, a planar section, a section with extension along a three-dimensional object, and on objects of four or more dimensions.

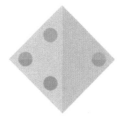

Pyramid of Perforation

A pyramidal container has perforation on the four triangular facets of the container. Each facet has between zero and three openings in the configuration of the vertexes of the equilateral triangles. Material can move through the openings of a facet and exit via the openings of one of the three connected facets.

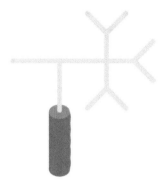

Branching Pipes on Handle

Pipes that branch are on a handle. The pipes bifurcate into three and then two pipes. The pipes can be put to the mouth. The length, diameter, and direction of the pipes, the number of branches, and the shape of the pipe network increases or decreases the pressure of air.

Chapter 9

Clothing & Accessories

Clothing science is the study of clothes, the fabrics and materials that clothes are made of, the properties of clothes such as insulation and porosity, and the interaction of clothes to the environment.

Accessories can be worn that are not clothes. Wristwatches, earphones, and VR headsets are accessories. Accessories might be attached at the wrist, head, or arms and legs via bands, sleeves, and straps.

Headgear is clothing worn on the head, such as hats, bandannas, headbands, and hairbands. Facial clothing can be face shields and veils. There is clothing for the torso, legs, arms, hands, and feet. Body suits can cloth most or all of the body.

Belts are circumferential bands that are worn around the waist. Sashes are bands that can be worn at many angles on the body. Bracelets, wristbands, and leg bands are bands around the arms, wrists, and legs. Rings are bands worn on the fingers.

A sleeve is an elongated band. Sleeves are sometimes individual to parts of the body. There are arm sleeves, leg sleeves, and finger sleeves. Sleeves can branch in a shirt from a tube at the torso or branch in pants from the waist to the legs.

Straps can be wrapped around the body. Bandannas and kerchiefs are wrapped around the head and scarfs are wrapped around the neck. Sheet cloth may be wrapped on the waist and over the shoulders. Ponchos are sheets with a central opening to put the head.

Materials can be layered on the body in particulates. The application of particulates can offer insulation and regulate the accumulation of perspiration. Paste and face paint are worn on the face and body.

Transfer of heat, water, and materials across clothing is regulated by the layers of clothing, buttons, shirt zippers, and components of the clothing. Clothing can be opened or closed when the components are opened or closed.

There are clothing accessories with light shielding such as welding helmets. Heat reflective suits reflect heat back to the environment. Air pressure suits maintain atmospheric pressure inside suits in water, non aqueous liquids, atmospheres of alternative composition, and vacuum.

Mechanical parts and motorized components may be integrated into clothing. Components of clothing can rotate, translate and revolve. Parts may be transported, stored, and configured in clothing.

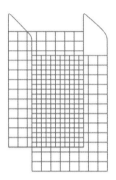

Grid Bar Vest

A vest with shoulder straps has grids of bars for the anterior and posterior sections of the vest. The interval between bars in rows and columns can be set to a size, such as 1 centimeter or 1 inch. The grid can be utilized for measurements and for positioning.

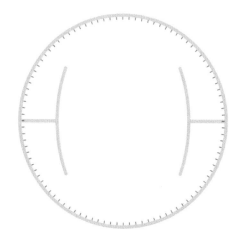

Centimeters on Ring of Headband

A headband with arcs to hold on to the temples has a connected ring with diameter equal to 30.83 centimeters and a circumference of 100 centimeters. The 100 centimeters are marked from right counterclockwise with inward rods.

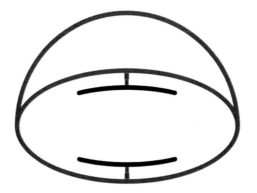

Band and Arcs

A hemispherical headband has a 360° band with a perpendicular 180° arc from the front to the back that is in the middle between the left and right of the headband. Forward on the headband is to the right. Arcs on spring rods press on both of the temples to wear.

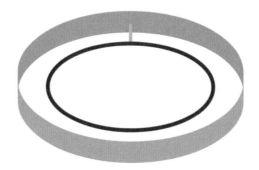

Headband and Vertical Torus

Headgear is clothing on the head, whether over all of the head, around the head, above the head from front to back, above the head from left to right, symmetric attachment, or another wrapping. A headband has a connected torus that is extended in height.

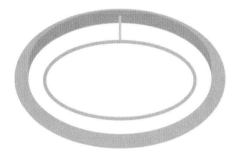

Headband and Torus with Groove

Circumferential structures on hats can be in many geometric shapes, sizes, and positions on a hat. A headband is held to a torus connected with a rod. The torus is concave. The torus has a groove on the inside circumference of the torus.

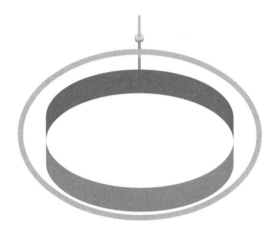

Hat with Ring

There can be moving parts on clothing accessories that are mechanical. A hat has a ring on a bead with an opening. The ring translates with the bead on a rod vertically, from the base of the hat to above the torus of the hat.

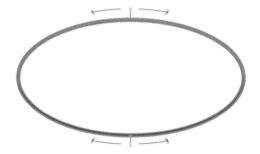

Rods on Motor

Electronic and motorized machines may be a part of accessories. A headband has two rods on a track that traverse with a motor. The track is circumferential. The rods can move or be stationary and operate sequences of motions in programs.

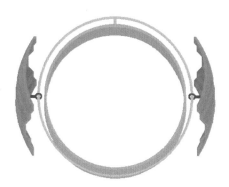

Headband with Arc Boards on Track

Tracks can be integrated into clothing and accessories. A headband with a circular track has arc boards that can transit. The track is a ring and the boards are connected to beads with openings that are attached to the track. The boards vary in width on angles.

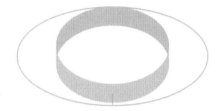

Hat with Elliptic Ring

Structures can be connected to headgear at the front, back, left and right sides, top, and circumferentially. A hat with a vertical torus has an elliptic ring that is held with rods. The elliptic ring is elongated to the forward at a length that is multiplied by two from the width.

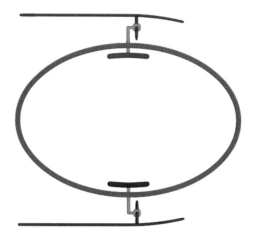

Headband with Rods on Beads

Moving parts can alter the shape of clothing accessories within a range of shapes and sizes. A headband with two pads has rods on the temples that translate laterally to the body when worn. The accessory expands and contracts in size.

Headband

A headband can be a loop or arc of band that is at the forehead or hair. The height of the edge of the top of a headband is in a wave pattern. The headband is a torus with a circular base and two wave crests in a loop at the top.

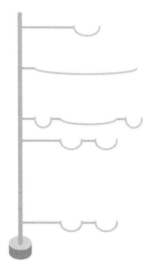

Structure of Bars

Bars curved in the shape of the body at five heights are held on a vertical rod. From top to bottom the bars mold to the head, torso and shoulders, chest and arms, thighs, and ankles. A person can stand in the curvature of the bars.

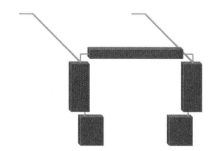

Headband and Plates

Frontal structures can be on a headband. There is a top
bar, temples, and temple tips on a headband. Plates are
on the front, connected via rods. The plates are on the
forehead and jaw region and extend outward of the
frontal area.

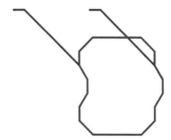

Face Wreath

The perimeter of the face can be set with bar edges on one to three dimensions. This face wreath has interconnected bars on the perimeter of the face that are along three dimensions, from forehead to chin and from the left to the right of the jaw.

Platforms on Rods

A man wears platforms in three columns. The platform on the left column can translate vertically on a rod. The second platform has three stationary platforms. The platform on the right can translate on a rod. The platforms may hold items and transport the items vertically.

Two-Layer Bracelet

Clothing and accessories can be in multiple layers. Layers may be for insulation, filtration, semi-permeable transport, and functions. A man is wearing a bracelet that has two layers of tubes. The tubes are held with rods in between.

Rows of Finger Holders

Two rows of finger holders are on the hand of a man. The finger holders are plates with openings in a row. The finger holder with four slots is proximal to the man and the finger holder with two slots is distal to him. When the man extends and flexes his fingers, moving one finger will move another finger or fingers.

Light Bulb in Bracelet

Lighting with light bulbs is a part of clothing and accessories. Bulbs on the front center of helmets are utilized in mining, construction, and spelunking. Light bulbs can be put inside clothing or on the surface of clothing. A light bulb is on the interior of a bracelet.

Tube Strapped on Shoulders

A man wears a tube on his back at the shoulders on straps. The tube is elongated in height and symmetrical. The shape of the tube is maintained along its length. The opening of the tube is from back to forward in the direction that the man is pointed.

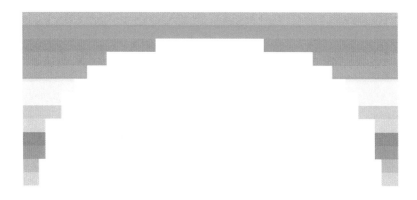

Chapter 10

Physical, Chemical, and Geological Systems

Rocks are formed from geological activity. Biogenic rocks form from deposits of biological material. Speleothems are rock formations in cave systems. Stalactites, stalagmites, flowstone, and coralloid are speleothems. Rock formations can be grown in the laboratory with crystals.

In physical environments, there is the composition, quantity, and processing of matter. Constructed processes occur in computation. A canal that opens and closes 1 per day may permeate liquids into an environment in regular patterns.

Stacks can open and close for periods. A stack with a valve that opens 1 hour per week to disperse gas can increase and decrease gas composition and atmospheric pressure in the atmosphere. Stacks can emit gases in designated proportions that benefit the ecosystem.

Calcium decreases the amount of CO_2 in the atmosphere. Calcium combines with CO_2 to form calcium carbonate. The CO_2 is removed from the atmosphere. A field of calcium with a folded topology to increase surface area would decrease the amount of CO_2 in the atmosphere. The size of the field that is open is increased if CO_2 concentrations increase and decreased if the CO_2 concentrations decrease.

Computational states in the environment may be a valve that is on or off, a water gate that is up or down, or a condenser set at a temperature for 1 hour per day. Some materials are allowed in and some materials are allowed out of a system to the environment.

In pertaining to chemicals in the environment, mixing of chemicals might occur in a succession of pools that flow into each other from increased elevation to decreased elevation, either linear or branched. Tunnels that diverge and converge process materials that flow along the length of the tunnels. Materials might be at different heights on a rock that is inundated with water from the tide. The materials dissolved for a period. A rock pushed and pulled by the tide in a groove may be a track. The height of the tide and the length of transit of the rock can be directly proportional.

Chemical configurations in geologic strata form states and computations. The configuration can be constructed. A steam can be bifurcated into two streams, then converge into one stream. A substance injector can be put on one of the two streams, one half distance along the stream. The injector inserts substance or not each day.

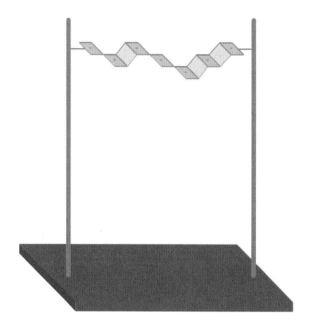

Stalactite Mold

A mold to grow a stalactite is on a pedestal held at a height with rods. The mold has containers with holes through which water may traverse to form a stalactite. In this mold the ceiling of the stalactite is at one of three heights.

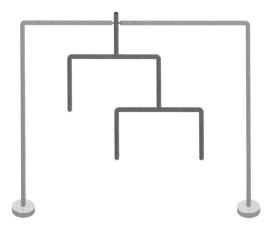

Branching Stalactite Mold

A mold on which a stalactite can grow is on a rack. The mold branches on rods. Water with suspended materials can flow on the branches of the mold. The material is then deposited into a stalactite. The mold has courses for the flow of material.

Water Circuit and Open System

A system that is open has interactions with the environment. A closed system does not input or output material. A water circuit with two containers for water has a valve between that can be turned on or off. There are two pipes with openings on the two sections of the container for interaction with the environment. The valve is set to alternate between open and closed 1 per hour indefinitely.

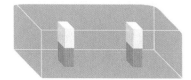

Heaters in Container of H2O

Two heaters are in a container of H2O. The temperature of each heater can vary over time according to algorithm. The container is open at the top to generate an open system. The temperature difference, if there is one, increases or decreases the mixing of chemicals and chemical reactions.

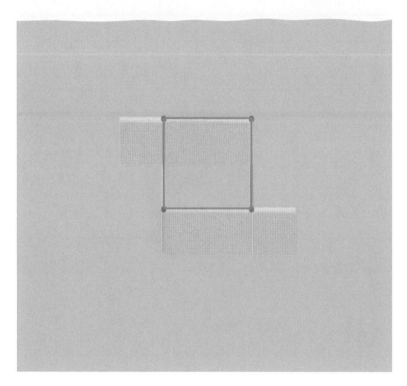

Input and Output in H2O

A 2 x 2 array of nodes has plates that can open for passage and connect for holding H2O and dispersed materials. Each node has two plates. The structure can close along the exterior, be open at each area, or open on some of the areas. A concentration of substances may be held for a time, then released.

Materials at Angle

Plates of materials A and B are at an angle in a holder. The materials from left to right are zinc and iron. Any solid can be put in the plate slots. If there is a liquid then it can be put in a container or if it is a gas then it can be put in a gas tank and then set in the slot. The magnetic field, temperature, and properties of the materials are in a spectrum of rotation.

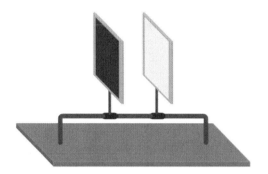

Plates of Elements at Distance

Two plate holders are on a bar and can move to varied distances from each other on a tube. Elements of the Periodic Table are in the holders. Graphite of the element carbon is in the left holder and platinum is in the right holder. Various elements can be put into the holders and set at a distance to each other that can be increased and decreased.

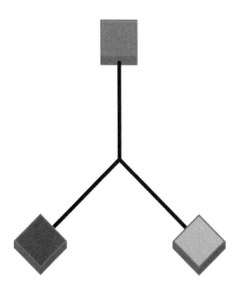

Containers of Materials

Three containers of materials are inserted in a network of bars that are 120° at three angles. The materials are from top and clockwise copper, aluminum, and iron. A number of materials can be put into the containers. The motion of the structure is based in part on the number and types of materials.

Gas Containers and Rail

Three containers of helium gas are connected with bars. A container of hydrogen gas is attached to a 180° arc rail. The hydrogen gas container can move on a bead on the arc rail. The motion of the structure is based in part on the type, moles, temperature, and volume of the gases and on the range of motion of the hydrogen gas container.

Array of Pins with Holders

A 3 x 3 array of pins are set in a board. The pins move forward and back. Holders can be moved along the pins and set to form a range for each pin to move. There can be one holder or not a holder on each side of the board. The pins are at the board on both sides for a stationary pin.

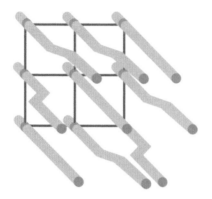

Array of Pipes

Mouthpieces can be a pipe or multiple pipes which can be in an array. A mouthpiece has a 3 x 3 array of pipe on bars that can be put to mouth. The pipes are either linear on their course or curve to the left or right. The pipes at the back are at equal intervals on two perpendicular dimensions.

Course of Elements

Plates of elements are connected along a course. From top to bottom and left to right the elements are carbon, manganese, gold, carbon, zinc, silver, iron, tin, and manganese. An object moving on the course engages in physical interaction with sequences of elements.

Pipes and Particulates

A pipe bifurcates into two pipes. The pipe on the left is composed of silicon and the pipe on the right is composed of nickel. The two pipes merge to form one pipe. Fluid is poured through the pipes. Some particulates of the solid materials of the pipes will be carried into the fluid. Silicon and nickel can be put into the fluid when the fluid is put through the pipes.

One-Dimensional Replication with Bars and Holders

A one-dimensional array of bars are inserted into a board with openings. The bars can extend through the openings. The bars are fastened with holders. The board and bars interact with a landscape and form into a shape with the bars which is complementary. The holders latch the shape. The board then interacts with another landscape to indent the shape.

About the Author

My name is David Elkins. I live in Oregon.

Made in the USA
Columbia, SC
02 July 2024

5dda304c-df3a-44f9-8c3e-bc3cbdb02c75R01